Ten Steps to a
BEDTIME STORY

William Essex

CLIMBING TREE BOOKS

First published 2010

This edition published 2022
by Climbing Tree Books Ltd.

www.climbingtreebookstore.com

Copyright © William Essex 2010, 2022

ISBN 978 1 909172 95 1

Cover design and typesetting by Grace Kennard

Cover artwork by
iStock.com/bgwalker & Grace Kennard

Inside illustrations by Grace Kennard

All rights reserved. No reproduction
permitted without the prior permission
of the publisher.

To B, B, B and C

Disclaimer

No animals, magical or otherwise, were harmed in the writing of this book. One frog was turned into a prince, but he's okay about that. The pony has a new stable and the scruffy little dog has been found a corner of the little boy's bedroom for his basket.

No resemblance is intended between any of the characters in this book and anybody out there in the real world. There's some nudity in the story (page 36) but you can't see much. It's okay. You can read this book in the presence of children.

Contents

The Early Days	9
The Ten Steps	13
Step One	13
Step Two	14
Step Three	15
Step Four	16
Step Five	17
Step Six	19
Step Seven	21
Step Eight	22
Step Nine	23
Step Ten	25
The all-important Bonus Step	27
The Emergency Story	30

The Early Days

Bedtime storytelling began when the first toddler refused to go to sleep without a story, and the first tired parent replied, "Once upon a time…"

Books hadn't been invented in those days, and this particular toddler had read through all the cave paintings too many times already.

In desperation, knowing that she only had two hours before the even newer baby woke up for the next feed, the first tired parent threw aside her charcoal wall-painting sticks, gave up hoping that her partner would stop pretending to be asleep, and just started talking.

Ten Steps to a Bedtime Story

—

And do you know—as the story went on, she began to enjoy herself. It was a good story, too, full of helpful mammoths, dinosaurs that went "squeak!" when you squeezed them, and lots of friendly things that only went bump in the night because they were trying to get comfortable.

That night, and over the nights that followed, the first tired parent discovered that the combination of her voice and a few reassuringly predictable adventures were better than anything else for getting her two-year-old to sleep.

The text of this book represents the distilled wisdom of many generations of tired parents. First deciphered from faint charcoal marks discovered on the walls of a prehistoric cave dwelling, it has been fully updated for the needs of the twenty-first-century tired parent.

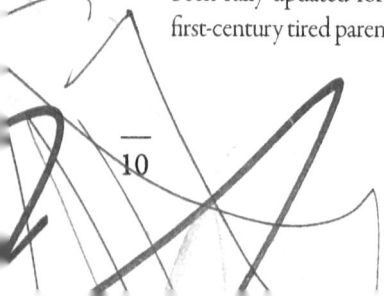

The Early Days

If you like the idea of telling your own bedtime stories, or even if you've just lost the usual storybook, all you have to do is, hide this book somewhere in your child's bedroom.

The idea is not to read it every time, but to have it handy as a means of kick-starting your own imagination. Use it to get started, and then put it aside as you tell your own story. [Just don't lose it. You might need it again.]

As the title suggests, this book works in steps. There are ten of them, plus one bonus step. There's also a story that develops step-by-step between the lines as the book goes on. If you're too tired to think, let alone tell a coherent story, turn to page 30. You'll find the whole of the developing story set out in one place, one version of it anyway, with additional details thrown in, for use in an emergency.

Ten Steps to a Bedtime Story
—

So let's get started. As soon as faces are washed, teeth brushed, cuddly toys found and restored to their owners, everybody tucked in and comfortable, we'll move on to ...

Step One

Always start a bedtime story the same way. "Once upon a time..." works perfectly well, as does just about anything else as long as it's consistent.

Your child will get the message that a story's coming and settle down. You will get yourself past the hump of wondering how to start.

If you like, you can start with a question. "What would you like the story to be about?" Audience participation in a children's story is a good thing, as long as you don't get too long a list of things to include.

And an alert child listening for the appearance of the flying pig won't get any sleepier until the pig is in sight. Same for all those other clever touches that sounded so good when you weren't actually trying to work them into the story.

Step Two

"Once upon a time there was a ..." what? Good choices are: little boy, little girl, dog, pony, teddy bear.

And give it some detail: a "scruffy little dog" or a "white pony with a long mane" or perhaps a "little green frog who was secretly a prince". The more detail you put in, the sooner the story will start to tell itself.

The Ten Steps

You know what's going to happen to that frog already, don't you?

Step Three

"...Called..."

Okay, called what? Wait for it.

If your child suggests a name, well done, you already have your child's attention and you might get some plot suggestions later.

If not, let's see; you could put in a name from TV or a film or a book, but if you want this to be your own story, how about something exotic and memorable?

Failing that, the first name that comes into your head. Failing even that, the first word. You won't be the first tired parent to tell a story about a scruffy little dog called Carpet.

Step Four

"...Who lived in..." a kennel or a castle or a spaceship or a pirate ship or a run-down old stable. Something appropriate to your leading character.

Again, the more detail you put in, the more the story takes over. The stable is leaky, is it? And cold? Does the pony need a new owner? Could that new owner be a child, perhaps?

And does the pony keep herself warm at night by dreaming that a kind little child is one day going to come and rescue her from this run-down stable?

Step Five

"One day..." Enough of this descriptive stuff. From now on, gentle action will hold the attention far better than description.

Start by setting the scene. For a small child, comfortably familiar is just as good as wildly creative. Predictable is good, too.

"One day, the scruffy little dog called Carpet was playing in the garden." Perhaps the frog was

Ten Steps to a Bedtime Story

rowing his lily pad around the lake. [Of course it's a free-floating lily pad and of course he's got a paddle. This is a children's story, remember?]

By the way, repetition can be really useful. "Once upon a time there was a little green frog who was secretly a prince... One day the little green frog who was secretly a prince was sailing his boat," and so on.

Don't overdo it, but repetition helps your voice develop a bedtime rhythm that will help with the getting to sleep. Frankly, it also helps you keep track of where you are in the story. [If you're stuck, children don't mind answering the question, "Where were we?" occasionally. If you're really stuck, you can follow it up with, "What do you think is going to happen next?"]

… **The Ten Steps**

Step Six

"...When..."

Okay, this is it. Action. This is when the thing happens that leads to the happy ending. It can be good or bad, but don't get carried away. Nothing that will wake up your child. When the puppy found a bone or met another puppy. When the frog's lily-pad sank. When the roof of the stable fell in.

Any time between here and Step Nine, feel free to repeat steps. You only need one cuddly teddy bear called Marmaduke who lived in a tree house, but if you're up to it, the more that happens in Marmaduke's world, the better.

Ten Steps to a Bedtime Story

Just don't waste time explaining what's going on. In a good children's story, things happen neatly, quickly and simply, one after another. The plot doesn't have to be logical (and sometimes it's better, and funnier, if it isn't).

In an emergency, if you've talked yourself into a tight spot, the word "Suddenly" can come in useful.

Suddenly a talking bird appeared and said, "There's a magic ring hidden in that hollow tree trunk. Why don't you find it?"

Suddenly, a talking squirrel popped its head out of the tree trunk and said, "Here it is. I've found it for you."

And then suddenly a fairy godmother appeared and said, "That's my ring. But I'll grant you the regulation three wishes if you give it back to me."

Probably worth mentioning again here that inviting audience participation is an effective way of holding the attention of a wakeful child.

What three wishes would you have, darling?

Step Seven

How did all of that feel?

If a bad thing's just happened, don't go further down the emotions than "the puppy was sad" or "very sad". We're going down to go back up, remember? Tears are good because crying animals in children's stories need to be hugged and kissed and settled down for sleep – and you can act that part out.

Lonely is pretty good, too, especially if your main character could conceivably be adopted as a pet. Try talking your way towards a love affair between a lonely cuddly toy/animal and a child in search of a pet. The story almost tells itself.

Step Eight

Action leads to reaction. I'd guess that frog is swimming to the shore. That pony has probably bolted out of the stable. Perhaps a child who wants a pet pony has come climbing over the nearest fence.

This is where a lot of the action of the story happens. Something's happened, and now it's being sorted out. The princess finds the soaking-wet frog, picks him up, and – no, no child would believe she'd do that willingly.

If you've had a really bad day and the ideas still aren't coming, it's time to cut straight to the L-word.

Here goes...

Step Nine

"Luckily..."

Ten Steps to a Bedtime Story
—

Look, this is storytelling for a small child, okay? And it's the end of a long day.

You might be flying solo by now, with the dog from next door contesting ownership of that bone, or the frog riding on the back of a fish that was secretly a princess, or the pony bolting into somebody's garden, but sooner or later, ideally before the thing gets too complicated, you're going to need the L-word.

Luckily, the bone had the dog's name on it. Luckily, the horse next door offered to share his stable. The thing about "Luckily" is that it slows things down to bedtime speed.

Luckily, your child's eyes have begun to close and you can lower your voice, speaking ever more softly now ...

Step Ten

Resolution.

Mummy says yes, the little girl can keep a pet pony in her bedroom.

The princess has a pond in her bedroom where the frog can live.

The friendly woodcutter you should have mentioned earlier comes in for his tea and offers to make a kennel for the puppy

Although in fact the puppy looks so much like a pillow that nobody notices him curled up in the child's bed.

Ten Steps to a Bedtime Story

So they all lived happily – but wait! What is this?

The Ten Steps

The all-important Bonus Step

Not that you're hinting or anything, but everybody GOES TO SLEEP at the end of a satisfactory bedtime story. Goes to sleep comfortably, quietly, and above all QUICKLY. So ...

"Good night."

"I want another story."

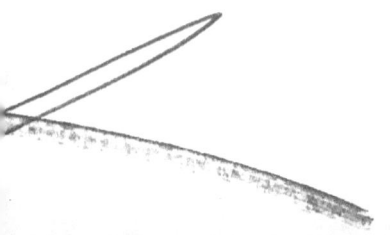

Ten Steps to a Bedtime Story

"You've just had a story. You can't have another one."

"But Teddy wants a story."

"Wasn't Teddy listening to any of that?"

"That was my story. Teddy wants her own story."

[Sigh. And because this is a book for grown-ups as well, we interrupt the narrative here for a brief daydream about the partner who puts his/her head around the bedroom door to whisper goodnight. Who offers to bring up a drink or a snack, or just possibly, who's just finished the washing-up and offers to take over. Unfortunately, this is the only paragraph in this whole book in which the frog almost certainly isn't a member of a royal family.]

The Ten Steps

"Okay, but this is positively the last story. You have to promise to go to sleep when it's finished."

"I promise."

"Okay. Let me see..."

Good luck! And above all – enjoy your story, and the telling of it.

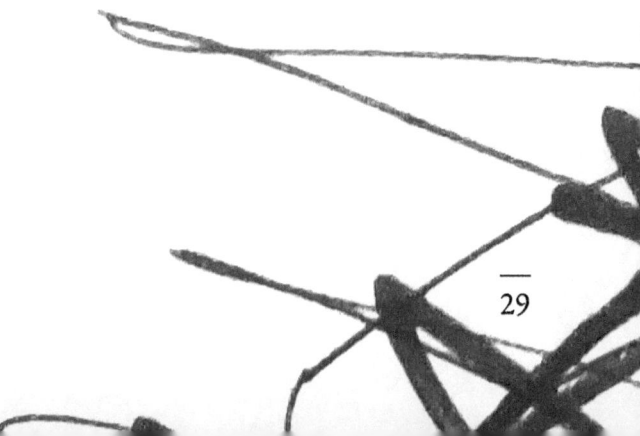

Ten Steps to a Bedtime Story

The Emergency Story

Once upon a time...

...there was a frog who was secretly a prince.

His name was Charmingson.

He lived in a wide green pond next to a big castle.

Now, the pond was full of lily pads and the frog spent all his time rowing around on his favourite lily pad, using an old plastic ice-cream spoon as a paddle.

The Emergency Story

One day, the frog was rowing around as usual, when he saw a little girl kneeling on the grass next to the pond and watching him. The little girl was wearing a long white dress and there was a silver crown on her head.

The dress, as you might expect, was very muddy.

"That's odd," thought the frog. "Usually they're dressed in shorts and tee-shirts and their parents are yelling at them not to fall in."

What the frog didn't realise was that today was a special day, and the castle was closed to the public. This meant that the little girl, who usually stayed in her room in one of the turrets, could come out and play without people pointing at her and wanting her autograph.

Ten Steps to a Bedtime Story

—

The little girl, as you will have realised by now, was a princess, and a famous one at that. Her name was Bella and she was frequently on television. She had a million followers, lots of toys in her room, and she could have friends around for sleepovers whenever she liked.

But sometimes, she just wanted to come and play in the garden.

"Hello," said the frog, rowing up to her.

"Hello," said Bella, kneeling back on her heels.

She was a polite little girl, and if she was surprised that a frog should row up to her on a lily pad and say hello, she didn't show it.

"Who are you?" said the frog, and Bella

The Emergency Story

explained about herself.

"Who are you?" she asked politely, when she had finished.

"I'm a prince," said the frog, and he told her a long, complicated story about how he had been bewitched by a wicked step-mother who turned him into a frog and then stole his bicycle.

"There was a prince who used to live here," said Bella. "It was before we moved in. His name was Charmingson. He disappeared."

"That was me!" said the frog. Then he stopped, as though he had just thought of something. He eyed the little girl's crown.

There was a silence. The little girl looked

33

thoughtful as well.

"I suppose you want me to kiss you," she said eventually.

The frog looked worried.

"We could close our eyes," he said.

Suddenly, there was a shout. Another girl came running towards them. She too wore a crown.

"Oh, no," whispered Bella.

"Who's that?" said the frog.

"That's my big sister. Her name's Nastia. She plays with my toys."

"She's a princess too, isn't she?" said the frog.

The Emergency Story

He and Bella looked at each other thoughtfully.

"What's that?" said Nastia, kneeling down next to Bella. "Is it a frog? Yeuch!"

"Yes, it is, look!" said Bella, and in one swift movement she picked up the frog in her hand and held it out towards Nastia. The frog leapt forwards and then there was a wet green kiss-shape planted right on Nastia's lips. The frog leapt back into the pond.

"Yeeuch! Splffpfthpppfthlurp!" shouted Nastia, and she ran away, spitting and wiping at her lips.

"Wow!" said Bella, watching her go. "That was really cool! That was–"

Ten Steps to a Bedtime Story

She stopped, and clapped her hand to her mouth in surprise.

Sitting waist-deep in the pond was a boy about the same age as she was. He too had a silver crown on his head.

"Ribit," said the boy. "Ribit, ribit!"

"Oh no!" said Bella.

But then the boy grinned. "Don't worry, I can still talk," he said. "But it's very cold in this pond and I haven't got any clothes on. Frogs don't wear clothes."

Luckily, there was a suitcase concealed in the bushes next to the pond. The suitcase contained clothes for a prince, and a towel with a crown

The Emergency Story

printed on it.

So Charmingson dressed while Bella looked the other way, and then Bella took him into the castle. Everybody was pleased to see him and lots of photographers came to put his picture in the news. The police were told to look out for a wicked stepmother on a bicycle and she was very soon arrested.

Then Charmingson and Bella played happily together until bed-time. They weren't able to do their teeth, because Nastia had locked herself in the bathroom with all the toothpaste and all the toothbrushes, but they both went to sleep straight away, without asking for extra stories, and they both had lovely dreams. So ...

"Good night."

By the Same Author

What do Mummy and Daddy do
while YOU are asleep?

Every year, Jemima says
"Can I come too, Daddy?"
This year, Father Christmas says "Yes!"

Holly Cool and the Time Machine

God - The Interview and other stories

The Journey from Heaven

The Book of Fake Futures

www.williamessex.com

www.ingramcontent.com/pod-product-compliance
Lightning Source LLC
Chambersburg PA
CBHW021453080526
44588CB00009B/838